ISRAEL
the land

Debbie Smith

A Bobbie Kalman Book
The Lands, Peoples, and Cultures Series

 Crabtree Publishing Company

www.crabtreebooks.com

The Lands, Peoples, and Cultures Series

Created by Bobbie Kalman

Coordinating editor
Ellen Rodger

Consulting editor
Virginia Mainprize

Project development, writing, editing, and design
First Folio Resource Group, Inc.
  Pauline Beggs
  Tom Dart
  Marlene Elliott
  Kathryn Lane
  Debbie Smith

Special thanks to
Shawky J. Fahel, J. G. Group of Companies; David H. Goldberg, Ph.D., Canada-Israel Committee; Steven Katari; Taali Lester, Israel Government Tourist Office; Alisa Siegel and Irit Waidergorn, Consulate General of Israel; and Khaleel Mohammed

Photographs
Steven Allan: p. 11 (both), p. 12, p. 14 (bottom left), p. 16, p. 18 (top), p. 21 (top), p. 28 (top); Lev Borodulin/Photo Researchers: p. 17 (top left); Van Bucher The National Adubon Society Collection/Photo Researchers: p. 25 (bottom right); Joel Fishman/Photo Researchers: p. 21 (bottom right); Baruch Gian/Consulate General of Israel: p. 17 (bottom); Louis Goldman/Photo Researchers: p. 8 (top), p. 19 (bottom); Tibor Hirsch/Photo Researchers: p. 19 (top); Israel Government Tourist Office: p. 8 (bottom), p. 14 (right), p. 15 (bottom), p.17 (top right), p. 30 (right), p. 31 (top); Rafael Macia/Photo Researchers: cover; Richard T. Nowitz: p. 3, p. 4–5, p. 7 (bottom), p. 9 (left), p. 10 (both), p. 14 (top left), p. 15 (top), p. 18 (bottom), p. 20, p. 21 (bottom left), p. 22 (top), p. 23, p. 24, p. 25 (bottom left), p. 26–27 (all), p. 28 (bottom), p. 30 (left), p. 31 (bottom); Richard T. Nowitz/Photo Researchers: p. 29; Mark D. Phillips/Photo Researchers: p. 9 (right); Eldad Rafaeli/Corbis: p. 13 (bottom); David Rubinger/Corbis: p. 13 (top); Jerry Shulman/Visual Contact: p. 22 (bottom); Inga Spence/Tom Stack & Associates: title page, p. 7 (top); Laura Zito The National Audubon Society Collection/Photo Researchers: p. 25 (top)

Map
Jim Chernishenko

Illustrations
William Kimber. The sabra, or prickly pear cactus, appears at the head of each section. An ibex, a wild goat native to Israel, is shown on the back cover.

Cover: A Roman aqueduct stretches along the beach at Caesaria.

Title page: A young man leads his donkey through the narrow streets of old Jerusalem.

Crabtree Publishing Company
www.crabtreebooks.com   1-800-387-7650

Cataloguing in Publication Data
Smith, Debbie, 1962-
Israel: the land / Debbie Smith.
p. cm. -- (Lands, peoples, and cultures series)
Summary: Introduces the history, geography, people, and economy of the state of Israel.
ISBN 0-86505-309-X (paper). -- ISBN 0-86505-229-8 (rlb.)
1. Israel--Description and travel--Juvenile literature.
[1. Israel.] I Title. II. Series.
DS107.5.S639 1999
956.94--dc21   LC 98-39913
                                                CIP

Published in the United States
PMB16A
350 Fifth Ave.
Suite 3308
New York, NY
10118

Published in Canada
616 Welland Ave.,
St. Catharines, Ontario
Canada
L2M 5V6

Published in the United Kingdom
73 Lime Walk
Headington
Oxford
OX3 7AD
United Kingdom

Published in Australia
386 Mt. Alexander Rd.,
Ascot Vale (Melbourne)
VIC 3032

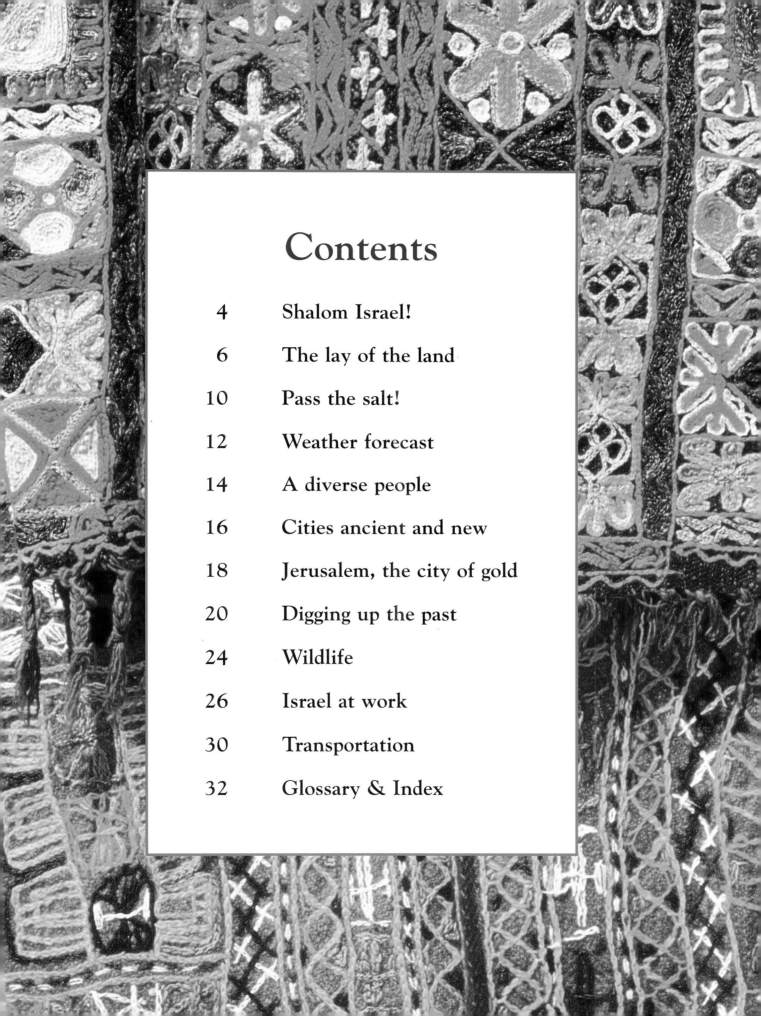

Contents

Shalom Israel!

As you stroll through a walled city in Israel or wind your way through a bustling marketplace, you will hear friends, neighbors, and relatives calling out to one another *"Shalom!" "Salam!"* These are the Hebrew and Arabic words for hello, good-bye, and peace.

In this country with little water and a lot of desert, people have wrestled with nature to build towns and cities, farms and factories. Israel is a modern country with an ancient history. The state of Israel was founded in 1948, but the land has been home to many groups of people over thousands of years. It is a center of worship for three major religions: Judaism, Islam, and Christianity. It is also a "homeland" and a dream come true for millions of people.

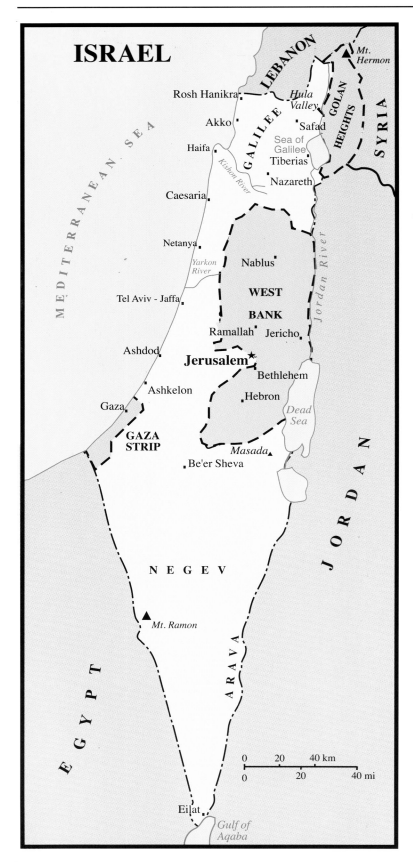

Israel is a sliver of land that is wedged between Jordan, Egypt, Lebanon, Syria, and the Mediterranean Sea. It is only 470 kilometers (290 miles) long and 135 kilometers (85 miles) wide. Its highest point, Mount Hermon, is a snowcapped mountain that rises to a dizzying height of 2814 meters (9219 feet). Its lowest point is the Dead Sea which plummets to an astonishing 400 meters (1312 feet) below sea level.

Israel's landscape is divided into four main geographical regions: the rift valley, the hills of Galilee, the coastal plains, and the Negev Desert.

A crack in the earth

Millions of years ago, the Earth's crust split and created a huge valley. This valley is known as the Great Rift Valley. It stretches from Syria in the north to Mozambique, in southern Africa, to the south. The Great Rift Valley follows a line along the entire eastern border of Israel. It passes through the Hula Valley, Sea of Galilee, Jordan Valley, Dead Sea, Arava Desert, and Gulf of Aqaba.

Israel's main inland waters are located in the Great Rift Valley. The longest river is the Jordan River. Its waters come from bubbling springs at the foot of Mount Hermon. As the Jordan River flows south, it feeds a lake known by three different names: the Sea of Galilee, Lake Tiberias, and Lake Kinneret. The Sea of Galilee is the largest lake in the country and the lowest lake in the world. It is also Israel's largest source of fresh water. Imagine an entire country getting most of its fresh water from one lake!

Emerald green farms, some with special fish-breeding ponds like the ones here, lie along the Jordan Valley.

The Great Rift Valley passes through the Arava Desert in the south of Israel.

The snowcapped peaks of Mount Hermon rise above Metulla, on the border with Lebanon.

The hills of Galilee

Steep cliffs, rolling hills, **fertile** valleys, and rivers cover the north and central parts of Israel. In the northwest, the limestone hills of Galilee drop into the sea. In the northeast stretch the Golan Heights, which were originally formed by ancient volcanic eruptions. Further south are rolling hills splashed with villages, olive groves, and **vineyards**.

The coastal plains

Many of Israel's first settlements were built on the coastal plains, which run along the Mediterranean Sea. Towns such as Jaffa and Akko became important port towns thousands of years ago. Today more than half of Israel's population lives in this region, with its white sandy beaches in the west and fertile farmland in the east.

Two friends enjoy a stroll through the surf of the Mediterranean Sea.

The Negev

The Negev is a large desert that is shaped like an upside-down triangle. The northern and southern parts are very different. The north is covered with low hills and plains. Here the soil is powdery, yellow, and fertile. The south is filled with **plateaus** covered with rocks and deep canyons that cut the landscape. There are dry riverbeds called *wadis* and huge craters called *cirques*. From time to time, fertile spots called oases pop up. The oases are fed by underwater springs that help trees such as the date palm and fig tree grow and bear fruit.

The waterfalls of Ein Gedi are a welcome relief from the scorching heat of the Judean Desert.

Millions of years of erosion have sculpted King Solomon's Pillars from red sandstone cliffs.

Pass the salt!

The Dead Sea, in the Judean Desert, is not a sea at all. It is actually a huge lake with the saltiest water in the world. At 400 meters (1312 feet) below sea level, it is also the lowest place on Earth.

The Dead Sea is fed mainly by the Jordan River. Once the water flows in, there is nowhere for it to go since water cannot flow upward and the Dead Sea is lower than the land around it. The trapped water **evaporates** in the heat and leaves salt and other minerals behind.

Swimming in salt

The Dead Sea is so salty that no fish or plants can survive in its waters. People swimming in the Dead Sea cannot sink. Instead, they bob around like corks. Some people believe that a float in the mineral-rich lake will make their aches and pains disappear. You have to be careful, though. The salt water stings and you may discover cuts that you never knew you had!

This child is covered from head to toe with warm, black mud from the Dead Sea. It takes the sting out of cuts and heals sore muscles and joints.

Because of all the salt in the Dead Sea, you can even sit up and read a magazine.

Harvesting the sea

The minerals from the Dead Sea are useful for more than healing bodies. Potash is used in **fertilizers** and **pesticides**. Bromine is used in the petroleum and chemical industries, in photography, and in medicine. Magnesium is used in fireworks and to build car and airplane parts.

(right) The Dead Sea Works produces potash for over 50 countries around the world.

(below) Salt from these deposits may one day end up on your dinner table!

Weather forecast

Israel has two main seasons: a rainy winter season that lasts from November to April and a dry summer season that lasts from May to October. The **climate** varies from region to region, depending on how high up you are and how far you are from the sea. The coolest spots are in the hills and mountains to the north. The hottest spots are in low-lying areas, such as on the shores of the Sea of Galilee and in the Arava Desert. The north and west parts of the country get the most rain. The driest places are in the south and in the east.

Temperature highs and lows

	January		August	
	High	**Low**	**High**	**Low**
Safad	9°C (48°F)	4°C (31°F)	29°C (84°F)	18°C (64°F)
Eilat	21°C (70°F)	9°C (48°F)	39°C (104°F)	25°C (77°F)

Rainfall highs and lows

	Average number of days	**Average amount of rainfall**
Safad	75	718 mm (28 inches)
Eilat	8	25 mm (1 inch)

Children laugh and scream as they soak each other with a water hose on a hot summer day.

A highway is suddenly swamped by a flash flood.

Flash floods

When a large amount of rain falls in a short amount of time, beware of flash floods! These floods rush down desert valleys and canyons. *Wadis* fill within minutes because the ground cannot absorb so much water. The floods are so powerful that they can uproot trees, shift boulders, and overturn cars.

*On a stormy day, a **sharav** tips over the lawn furniture and threatens to blow away the washing.*

Hold onto your hats!

A scorching wind blowing in from the Arabian Desert makes temperatures soar from May to June and again from September to October. This wind, called a *sharav* in Hebrew and a *chamsin* in Arabic, can last from two to five days at a time. The *sharav* is so hot and dry that it destroys flowers and burns stalks of ripening wheat. Even the cows are affected by the heat. They produce almost 15 percent less milk than usual unless they are in air-conditioned barns.

13

A diverse people

The people of Israel are as different and distinct as the country they live in. Some have lived on the land for generations. Others have **immigrated** to Israel from around the world.

Jews

Most Israelis are Jewish. Their religion, Judaism, is based on ten commandments, or laws, recorded in the Torah, the first five books of the holy Bible. The most important teaching is that there is only one God.

Jews first lived in Israel over 3000 years ago. As different **empires** conquered the land, most Jews were **expelled** to other countries. Many faced great hardship, and they prayed that they could one day return to their ancient **homeland**. About 100 years ago, the first wave of Jewish immigrants arrived in Israel from Europe. Other European Jews followed, as well as Jews from north Africa and various countries in the Middle East. Jewish immigrants continue to arrive in Israel today, many of them leaving hardship to return to their homeland.

(below) **Sabra,** *which means prickly pear, is the nickname given to people born in Israel. They are said to be prickly on the outside and soft on the inside, just like the fruit.*

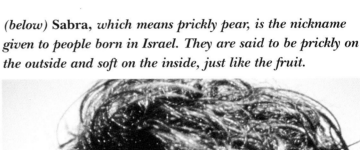

(above) Jews from Ethiopia came to Israel in the 1980s and 1990s to escape war and famine in Africa.

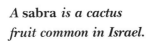

A **sabra** *is a cactus fruit common in Israel.*

Arabs

Arabs make up 15 percent of Israel's population. They ruled the country 1500 years ago and have lived there ever since. Most Arabs are Muslims. They follow the religion of Islam and live according to the word of God, Allah, and the teachings of the **prophet** Muhammad. Muhammad received instructions from Allah on how to lead a good life. These instructions are written in the Qur'an, the Muslim holy book. Other Arabs are Christians. They follow the teachings of Jesus Christ, known to Christians as the Son of God. His life and lessons are recorded in the New Testament, the Christian holy book.

Before Israel became a country in 1948, the land was called Palestine. Today, many of Israel's Arabs still call themselves Palestinians.

These Bedouin women wear the traditional clothing of their nomadic culture.

*This Arab man wears a **kaffiyeh** to protect himself from the scorching sun.*

Occupied Territories

When Israel declared its independence in 1948, the neighboring Arab countries declared war. Many Arab residents of Palestine left their homes during this war, called the War of Independence. Many of them settled in areas of Jordan, Egypt, Syria, and Lebanon that were close to the new country of Israel. Others remained in areas of Palestine that became part of Israel.

After the Six Day War in 1967, Israel took possession of areas in the neighboring Arab countries where many Palestinians were living: the Sinai Desert, the Golan Heights, the Gaza Strip, the West Bank, and East Jerusalem. These are considered to be the "Occupied" or "Administered" Territories. Israel returned the Sinai Desert to Egypt after a **peace treaty** was signed in 1979. In 1993, the Palestinians, who are hoping to create their own state in the West Bank and the Gaza Strip, were given control of parts of these areas in a peace accord. They are still waiting for the homeland that was promised to them.

Cities ancient and new

Some of Israel's cities are so old that you can see **synagogues**, **mosques**, streets, and city walls from hundreds, even thousands, of years ago. Other cities were once agricultural areas that grew as more and more people came to farm the land. Today new cities, called development towns, are being built so that immigrants and **refugees**, who continue to arrive in Israel, have a place to live and work.

Haifa, a port city

Haifa is located on the slopes of Mount Carmel and looks out over Haifa Bay. The center of Israel's technology industry, it is built on three levels. The port is on the lowest level. Shops, offices, restaurants, and older residential areas are on the next level up. The top level has many new neighborhoods, as well as some stores and restaurants.

Tel Aviv-Jaffa, the city that grew

The port town of Jaffa, on the Mediterranean Sea, is one of the oldest towns in the world. It is even mentioned in the Bible as the place from which Jonah set out, only to be swallowed by a whale.

In 1909, 60 Jewish families from Jaffa moved just outside of town. They founded the suburb of Tel Aviv. The suburb grew and grew until, in 1950, Tel Aviv-Jaffa became one city. Tel Aviv is the country's most important business center and is also the hub for shopping, theater, and sports. The busy Dizengoff Street is one of the best-known streets in Israel. In fact, in the Hebrew-language version of Monopoly, the name "Dizengoff" is used instead of "Boardwalk." Jaffa is the place to go if you want to visit galleries, cafés, and antique stores.

Massive container tankers, ocean liners, and cargo boats dock at the port in Haifa.

(left) Crowds bustle through the streets of Tel Aviv.

(below) Drivers would have a hard time squeezing through the narrow streets of Jaffa.

Be'er Sheva, the capital of the Negev

Be'er Sheva, in the northern part of the Negev, is built on a site that is over 3500 years old. The city bustles with stores, museums, and university students, but is best known for its colorful Bedouin market.

Every Thursday morning hundreds of Bedouin gather at Be'er Sheva's market to sell clothes, spices, arts and crafts, and even sheep and goats.

Jerusalem, the city of gold

Jerusalem, Israel's capital city, is a mixture of cultures, religions, languages, and **traditions**. Over 3000 years old, it is considered to be a **sacred** place by Jews, Muslims, and Christians. Jerusalem is divided into two parts: the old walled city and the new city outside the walls.

The Old City

The magnificent stone walls surrounding the Old City were built over 400 years ago. Eight gates lead into this part of Jerusalem which is divided into four quarters: Jewish, Muslim, Christian, and Armenian. The old city's narrow, twisty roads are packed with small homes, markets, and shops. All the buildings are made of a rose-gold stone, called Jerusalem stone, that makes the city glow at night. Many of Jerusalem's most sacred sites are in the Old City.

(right) The Church of the Holy Sepulcher was rebuilt 800 years ago on the ruins of an earlier Christian church.

The Dome of the Rock is sacred to Muslims. It marks the site from which the prophet Muhammad is believed to have risen to heaven for one evening to meet with Allah.

Outside the walls

Outside the Old City is a vibrant modern city. The first neighborhoods were built outside the walls over 100 years ago. Today the area includes office buildings, stores, restaurants, museums, and Israel's parliament, the Knesset.

(opposite) The Western Wall, also known as the Wailing Wall, is all that remains of the Second Temple. This Jewish holy site was destroyed by the Romans in 70 A.D. Every day Jews pray at the Western Wall. They slip prayers written on scraps of paper between the cracks of the wall in the hope that their prayers will be answered.

A major highway system runs just nine meters (30 feet) from the walls of the Old City.

Digging up the past

Archaeologists are explorers who seek out clues that tell how people lived, played, and worked in the distant past. They dig carefully through layers of earth and sand to find pots, weapons, works of art, and the remnants of buildings and towns. Israel has more than 3500 archaeological sites where people have uncovered mysteries of past civilizations.

The archaeological site of Tel Hatzor, in the north of Israel, has more than 20 layers of towns and villages from almost 3000 years of civilization.

"Tel" all

Tels look like rounded hills popping out of flat plains, but when archaeologists start digging they find much more than just dirt. They discover towns that were built on top of each other over many centuries. Each town was abandoned, and sand and dust covered the houses and garbage left behind. Many years later, another town would be built in the same location. As archaeologists study a *tel's* layers, they learn how the culture of a people changed over time.

Qumran

In 1947, a Bedouin shepherd boy was looking for his goat in a high hillside cave in Qumran, overlooking the Dead Sea. There he found some old jars with curious ancient scrolls. They were 2000-year-old manuscripts. The manuscripts included the oldest surviving copies of the Bible and the writings of the people who lived in Qumran. Over the next nine years, archaeologists continued to dig. They found over 500 manuscripts in eleven caves. These manuscripts are known as the Dead Sea Scrolls.

Archaeologists **excavated** below the caves and found aqueducts, or channels for transporting water, and cisterns, which are tanks that hold water. They also discovered a kitchen, an assembly hall, council chambers, a pottery workshop, and the room where the scrolls were written.

These archaeologists use hand picks to break through layers of rock. They are careful not to destroy an important finding.

Scholars today are putting together pieces of the Dead Sea Scrolls that disintegrated over time.

Look carefully at this desert scene. Can you see the caves where the Dead Sea Scrolls were discovered?

Masada

Masada is the site of two ancient palaces built as part of a fortress by the Roman governor Herod the Great almost 2000 years ago. The ruins are located on a mountain above the Dead Sea, 48 kilometers (30 miles) from Jerusalem. The fortress was taken over by Jews fleeing the Romans in 66 A.D. They lived there until the Romans recaptured Masada six years later.

The Romans set up eight camps around the base of Masada and built a ramp out of earth to the fortress walls. After eight months, they finally broke through the walls. Rather than surrendering, the Jews set fire to their homes and possessions and killed themselves. When the Romans captured the fortress the next morning, they found only two women and five children alive. The survivors had been hiding in a water pipe. Today you can visit the remains of Masada's palaces, swimming pools, lookout towers, and the oldest synagogue in the world.

(above) To reach the ruins of Masada, you can take a cable car to the top, hike up the winding Snake Path, or climb the much easier Roman Ramp.

The walls near this lookout spot on Masada are covered with beautiful patterns.

Caesaria

Herod the Great began building the city of Caesaria on the Mediterranean coast in 22 B.C. Archaeologists have uncovered remains of the many different civilizations who lived in this area before, during, and after Herod's time. The ruins of a hippodrome, an ancient Roman track used for racing horses and chariots, lie between two modern roads. Roman aqueducts that once brought water to Caesaria from a nearby spring run along the ocean. A large moat and massive walls surround the remains of an ancient city, where the foundations of a Christian cathedral can still be seen. Outside the ancient city is a **Byzantine** street paved with marble slabs and protected by two headless marble statues.

Arched tunnels lead into the restored Roman amphitheater in Caesaria, where visitors today enjoy concerts, plays, ballets, and operas.

Wildlife

A large variety of plants and animals make their home in Israel. Wildflowers of all kinds grow in the hills to the north where mountain gazelles roam. Bushy-tailed foxes and jungle cats travel the woods. Chameleons, gekkos, snakes, and other reptiles thrive in the desert where small shrubs and bushes grow.

Adapting to the desert

Plants in Israel have learned to **adapt** to the long dry spells in the Negev. Some seeds lie in the soil for years, waiting for a rainy winter before they all shoot up. Many trees and plants have deep roots so that they can search for water far underground. Small leaves on shrubs cut down on the amount of water that evaporates from the plant.

What happened to the trees?

Over 3000 years ago, Israel was covered with oak, pine, and terebinth trees. By the early 1900s, most of these trees had disappeared. Armies had chopped them down to use as firewood and to prevent enemies from finding cover. Farmers had cleared away trees to make room for farmland and grazing pastures for their animals.

In the early 1900s, the Jewish National Fund (JNF) was founded to buy land for new farms and forests. Since then, the JNF has planted more than 200 million trees, mostly pine and cypress. These trees help secure the soil so that wind does not blow it away. The trees also provide homes to small animals.

Bird watching

There are over 380 species of birds in Israel. Some live there through the year. Others spend their winters in Israel's mild climate. Birds such as eagles, falcons, and hawks nest in Israel. The best seasons for bird watching are the spring and fall, when over 500 million migrating birds pass over the country. Pelicans, storks, honey buzzards, and sparrow hawks are just some of the odd and beautiful birds that soar through the sky.

Protecting nature

Israel is trying to protect its wildlife. The government passed laws making it illegal to pick even the most common flowers. Over 150 **nature reserves** protect hundreds of plants and animals, including oak and palm trees, gazelles, ibexes, leopards, and vultures. Bird migration routes are monitored, and airplanes are forbidden to fly along these paths.

Wildlife biologists are trying to preserve or bring back plants and animals that were mentioned in the Bible. These scientists search around the world for animals such as the white oryx antelope, addax antelope, Asiatic wild ass, and ostrich. They bring these animals to special reserves in Israel where the animals learn to survive in the natural environment and are then set free.

Beautifully colored fish swim through the coral reefs in Eilat.

Storks rest on a beach before continuing their migration.

Some of the olive trees in the Garden of Gethsemane, in Jerusalem, are believed to be almost 2000 years old.

An ibex snacks on grass in a desert oasis.

Israel at work

Israel's economy has changed a great deal since it first became a country in 1948. Agriculture has always played an important part, but today Israel is becoming known for its research in science and technology, especially in the areas of farming, medicine, and computers.

Creating fertile farmland

Israel was once a country with poor land for farming. The good soil had washed away and the country was covered with rocks, deserts, and swamps. Water was scarce.

When Jewish settlers came to the country in the late 1800s, they began to clear the land. They drained marshes, removed rocks, and built wide flat rows called terraces in hilly regions so that when it did rain, the water did not wash the soil from the hills. They also developed **irrigation** systems to carry the little water that they had to their crops.

Scientists and farmers have continued to work together to find ways to increase the amount of water and to distribute it throughout the country. The National Water Carrier was built in the 1950s and 1960s. This system of huge pipes, canals, reservoirs, tunnels, dams, and pumping stations carries water from the north and central parts of the country to the south. New techniques have been developed to take salt out of sea water so that people can drink it or use it to water their crops. City sewage is also being purified so that it can be used for irrigation.

From the earth

Because of the various weather and soil conditions in different parts of the country, Israel grows a range of produce. Avocados, guavas, mangos, kiwis, and citrus of all kinds are planted in the coastal plains. Apples, pears, and cherries grow in the cooler hills to the north. Tomatoes, cucumbers, peppers, zucchini, and melons are harvested in the valleys. Bananas and dates thrive in the heat of the northern Negev Desert. Much of this produce is exported to countries around the world.

Israel grows flowers for export, including carnations, roses, and tulips.

Israeli farms

Very few farms in Israel are owned privately. Most farmers live on a *moshav*. A moshav is a small, self-contained village in which each family has its own field and home. The moshav often provides families with farming equipment and supplies, and markets everyone's produce.

Other farmers live on a *kibbutz*. The word kibbutz means "coming together." The members of a kibbutz share in the decisions, the work, the food, and the earnings.

(above) You may be able to buy oranges from Israel in your grocery store. Look for the brand name "Jaffa."

(left) Drip irrigation helps to conserve water. Long plastic tubes with small feeder holes are laid on the ground near the stems of plants. Computers are programmed to feed just the right amount of water and nutrients, drip by drip, through these holes to the plants' roots.

Tourism

Israel's history, beaches, sun, music, and food attract more than two million tourists every year. Many of these visitors are **pilgrims** who come to pray, learn, and visit the holy sites. Others are tourists who come to see relatives, celebrate the holidays, or work on a kibbutz for the summer.

Technology

The land of Israel does not have a lot of natural resources, but the people of Israel are very resourceful! They sell new ideas and technologies to countries around the world. Electronic machines used in hospitals, computer hardware, and software, agricultural technologies, and airplane parts all come from Israel.

Tourists strike a deal with a street merchant in Jerusalem.

Scientists in Israel have developed magnetic resonance imaging (MRI) systems that are used in hospitals and clinics.

A diamond in the rough

Israel is well-known for its diamond industry. Skilled and talented diamond cutters from Belgium and Holland made their way to Israel after World War II. In the 1950s, they began **importing** rough diamonds from Asia and Africa, cutting the diamonds into all shapes and sizes, and polishing the stones. Now Israel is the world's leading **exporter** of polished diamonds. Most of the diamonds are used in jewelry, but some are used in drilling and cutting machines.

Salt water pools near the Dead Sea absorb and store energy from the sun's rays. This energy is used to run small power plants.

Energy from the sun

Israel's main sources of fuel are oil and coal. Both of these resources are very expensive because they have to be imported. There is one energy source that Israel has plenty of – the sun. Many families heat their water by solar energy. In fact, it is a law that each new home must have a solar water heater. Collectors, which are water tanks with large glass plates, are placed on the roof. Collectors absorb the heat from the sun and warm the water. Three hours of sunshine a day is enough to provide hot water for a family of four. Even in winter, there is so much sunshine that other sources of heat, such as electric heaters, are rarely needed.

Because Israel is such a small country, it does not take long to travel from place to place. You can drive across the entire width of the country in an hour and a half and the entire length of the country in six hours.

Egged

Egged is the name of Israel's main bus network. It is a cooperative, which means that it is owned by its workers. Egged was formed in 1933, before there was a state of Israel. There were few highways at the time and the buses carried passengers, newspapers, mail, food, and general supplies. Today, Egged is the second largest bus company in the world. Four thousand buses travel between and within cities in Israel. Do not look for an Egged bus from about 3 p.m. each Friday to sunset on Saturday. Egged buses do not run on the Jewish Sabbath because it is a day of rest. They also do not run on Jewish holidays.

Taxi Please!

The *sherut* is a shared taxi that holds up to seven passengers. If you take a *sherut*, you will usually have to wait until it is full before you leave. The *sherut* travels along a specific route, between towns and cities, for a set price. You can get out along the way, but you still have to pay the full price. *Sheruts* also run in some cities. They take the place of buses that do not run on the Sabbath. There are also private taxis that are not shared, but they are usually very expensive.

Honk! Honk! Imagine being caught in this traffic jam at the beach in Tel Aviv.

Road signs show the way in Hebrew, Arabic, and English.

Fill 'er up! Donkeys come in useful when your car runs out of gas.

Camels are still used for travel in the desert. This camel needs a bit of a pull to get moving.

Glossary

adapt To adjust to new conditions

amphitheater A theater in the shape of an oval or circle, with levels of seats rising from a stage. Concerts and plays are held in amphitheaters.

Bedouin An Arab of the nomadic tribes that roam the desert in Israel

Byzantine Empire A branch of the Roman Empire that existed from the fourth to fifteenth century

climate The usual weather condition of a particular place, including temperature, rainfall, and humidity

empire A group of countries under one ruler

erosion The gradual washing away of soil and rocks by wind, fast-moving water, and glaciers

evaporate To change from a liquid into a gas. Clouds and mist are evaporated water.

excavate To uncover by digging

expel To order or force to leave a country

export To sell goods to another country

famine An extreme shortage of food in a country

fertile Producing or able to produce abundant crops or vegetation

fertilizer A material added to the soil to make it produce more crops

homeland A country that is identified with a particular people or ethnic group

immigrate To come to settle in a different country

import To buy goods from another country

irrigation The supplying of water to land using ditches, sprinklers, and other means

mosque A sacred building in which Muslims worship

nature reserve A place where animals and plants can live undisturbed by people

nutrient A substance that living things need in order to grow

peace treaty An agreement that is signed by two or more warring countries to end hostility

pilgrim A person who makes a religious journey to a sacred place

plateau An area of flat land that is higher than the surrounding land

pesticide A chemical that is used to kill harmful insects

prophet A person who is believed to speak on behalf of God

refugee A person who leaves his or her home or country because of danger

sacred Having special religious significance

synagogue A Jewish place of worship

traditions Customs that are handed down from one generation to another

vineyard An orchard where grapes are grown to make wine

 # Index

2 3 4 5 6 7 8 9 0 Printed in the USA 5